# Living Clay

# Living Clay

PRISCILLA HOBACK

with photographs by Jack Kotz

SHERMAN ASHER Publishing

Acknowledgments:
Cover Photography by Jack Kotz
Cover Design by Janice St. Marie
Book Design by Janice St. Marie and Judith Rafaela
Photography: Daniel Bansotti, p. 95; Ray Belcher, pp. 47, 89; Richard Dillingham, p. 64;
Family Archives pp. 25, 26, 79; Priscilla Hoback, pp. 45, 45, 56-57, 57, 69, 75, 83, 88; Fran Hogan, p. 64;
Jack Kotz, pp. 18-19, 53, 54, 54, 58-59, 59, 73, 74, 76-77, 78, 80, 80, 81, 82, 82, 83, 89, 90, 91, 97, 98-99;
Denise Lynch, p. 41; Otis Ombodin, p. 42; Robert Nugent, pp. 39, 65, 66

FIRST EDITION
Printed in Canada
ISBN 1-890932-14-0

Library of Congress Cataloging-in-Publication Data

Hoback, Priscilla, 1939-
    Living clay / by Priscilla Hoback.
        p. cm.
    ISBN 1-890932-14-0 (softcover)
    1. Pottery craft—New Mexico. 2. Clay. I. Title.

TT919.7.U62 N62 2000
738--dc21

                                            00-025215

**Sherman Asher Publishing**
PO Box 2853
Santa Fe, NM 87504
*Changing the World One Book at a Time*™

*For Rosalea, Denise, and Joseph*

*generations of blood—generations of spirit*

# CONTENTS

# INTRODUCTION

There has never been a major civilization that did not have an important tradition in ceramics. Through the centuries people have fired clay and made objects that remain with us to this day—from Egyptian faience to the porcelains of China and Limoges to the native pottery of America.

Priscilla Hoback has carved a niche for herself in the world of ceramic art. She has built a reputation usually reserved for the likes of Hamada, Cardew, Nampeyo and Maria Martinez. Priscilla has taken a different path, however, with the emphasis on her murals. In a stunning progression she is always changing, always evolving, from the utilitarian beginnings of her work—the bowls, cups, and platters—to the present works, which are truly works of art.

Even though I've known Priscilla and her art for many years she still amazes me with some new vision or technique. In addition to being an artist she is a born teacher. *Living Clay* is a way for her to teach and share with other artists and with her collectors. It's a lovely book, very evocative of Priscilla, New Mexico, and her very special art. I hope you enjoy it as much as I do.

—Nedra Matteucci

# FOREWORD

Priscilla Hoback transcends labels. Her life experiences form a foundation for her creative expression and personal philosophy—a spiritual evolution grounded in the earth itself and the animal subjects she knows so well. Thinking of the role that animal spirits play in her visual images, I am reminded of a favorite piece from her lynx series in the mid 1990's. Desert Cat, a cautious wild feline representative of the wild cats still living in the Ortiz Mountains near Galisteo, speaks of her own place in an ever changing landscape. "I see shadow cats in many colors, spotted with yellow eyes that reflect blue sky and purple mountains," she told me. "They are like me, watching the gold mines scar the mountain... the desert filled with people. Together, we gaze across the sands of that ancient sea bed to see the future coming—coming and changing our lives."

Her work, like her persona, defies stereotypical artistry. Whether etched in clay or inked on paper, her bold imagery seamlessly blends the old and the new, the archaic with the modern. Inspired by the timeless glyphs scattered throughout northern New Mexico, Hoback uses a powerful, engaging, and yet thoroughly modern sense of narrative expression channeled through an ancient medium.

The clay murals are evocative of man's earliest artistic expression, the Paleolithic cave art that has intrigued art historians and scholars for more than a century. Her clay surfaces with their early coloration and animal imagery are reminiscent of the painted walls discovered in recent times at Lascaux, Le Portel, and other sites throughout western France and the Iberian peninsula. Like these prehistoric drawings, Hoback's work portrays primarily animal imagery. Jean Clottes' account of the importance of animal representations in European Paleolithic art could just as well describe Priscilla's work today:

> Above all, Paleolithic art, from the beginning to end, is an art of animal forms.... Our first and lasting perception of this art is primarily that of a bestiary, both plentiful and diverse yet stylistically recognizable.
>
> — JEAN CLOTTES, *The Shamans of Prehistory*

Early man, Clottes goes on to say, "painted not a 'real' horse but a distorted horse, perhaps a 'spirit horse.'" Like her forerunners, Hoback strives to capture the essence of her animals, and whether depicting celestial bears or unbridled horses, this Galisteo artist, too, portrays "spirit animals." In doing so, she stretches our imagination and opens our minds to an exciting range of elements—exploration, process, creativity.

Wanting to know more about her process, I sat in on a workshop that Priscilla led at Santa Fe Clay. Ready to begin her demonstration, she approached the virgin clay slab,

*The Governor's Horses,*
*State of New Mexico's*
*Governor's Gallery, 1997*

observing it carefully, running her hand over it, noticing the character of its surface. As she observed, the composition emerged in her mind, and gradually she began to draw lightly in the clay, always following the natural characteristics of the rolled slab.

In allowing the medium to direct her composition, Hoback's process again mirrors that of the ancients. She incorporates

*Earth Dancers, 1998*
*Brown & Williamson*
*Corporate Headquarters*

cracks and nodules, hollows and bulges into an emerging work as did the early shamanistic artists who are thought to have followed the natural features of the cave's wall. Put more succinctly, "her figures inhabit the terracotta in an organic way. Somehow they seem naturalized within the environment of the clay," says my friend art historian John Clarke.

Uniting imagery and medium, Hoback provides a highly tactile, sculptural dimension, one that invites us to explore. As viewers, we find ourselves irresistibly drawn to the textured surfaces, wanting immediately to recreate the artist's own movements, to touch the stone, to run our fingers along rough edges and choppy surfaces, to absorb both process and dialogue. It is at this point that we realize the artist has masterfully meshed the ancient and the modern. But, unlike the ancients, her work encompasses a pure narrative which engages our curiosity. Is it a dance? we ask. Or is it a struggle, or perhaps both? Always maintaining a sense of realistic representation, she playfully uses movement and perspective to create her unique story.

Priscilla's narrative has intrigued my friend Tim Albright, a Mayan scholar, since he first discovered her murals. Many hearty discussions have found us agreeing that her work transcends well-structured rules. Tim points out that Hoback gives us

> "a thin slice of her narrative understanding of the herd's movement, one second frozen in time. The observer immediately assumes there is a story, with past actions and future potentials. [This] snapshot has captured 'movement' ...what this movement may be is open to interpretation. In this sense, her work combines a profound Realism... [with] a sense of gentle detachment reminiscent of Surrealism."

As *Living Clay* reveals, Priscilla Hoback is a woman of great independence, a modern woman—yet one who is relentlessly drawn to the sanctity and rituals of tradition. From building her own kilns and quarrying her own clay to tirelessly observing the animals she so aptly portrays, she has immersed herself in the evolution of her art. She instinctively knows the animals she depicts—horses, bears,

*Priscilla Hoback is a woman of great independence, a modern woman— yet one who is relentlessly drawn to the sanctity and rituals of tradition.*

wildcats, geese—knows them as animals, and the graceful realism of her figurative depictions reveals her extraordinary understanding of both their physiology and psyche.

Watching Priscilla move from one series to another over the last ten years, I have been awed by the depth of her personal creativity. External experiences provide inspiration, but it is her inner desire to push herself artistically and to draw from the early medium whose language she so fluently speaks that fuels her creative expression. It is always an enormous treat to visit her in Galisteo, to see what has recently been fired, or to hear tales that inspired a new series. Her murals are constantly evolving as she "pursues clay to new dimensions." I have come to expect and relish the magical hint of surprise. Perhaps it is her personal touch of the mythical Mercury, ever the trickster, that captivates our attention and keeps us anxiously awaiting the new.

—JUDITH TAYLOR
GALLERY AT SHOAL CREEK
APRIL, 2000

*Priscilla on the studio portal in Galisteo*

## AUTHOR'S NOTE

The land here in the Galisteo Basin of New Mexico is simultaneously primal, rural, and contemporary. Cattle and antelope graze near my farm, the sky swirls with billowing thunderclouds, choreographed dances of turkey vultures, and vapor trails of jet airplanes. Glyphs, crosses, brands, initials, and graffiti cover the rock escarpment that surrounds this basin. It has been marked by human hands from ancient origins to the tumultuous present. I too record my life here—gathering, shaping, and firing these clays. I feel life force manifest in this desert and claim a kinship with its diverse mineral kingdom. These natural clays are more than geology—they carry great beauty and inspiration, and form the unique nature of this region.

Before I moved here I envisioned the kiln I would build, one capable of holding temperatures exceeding those endured when rockets reenter earth's atmosphere; a kiln that would transform these ancient clays into a new geology of stone. But I did not know what living here was to mean to my work.

"May your roads meet" is an ancient blessing I was given. Forty years of clay work that included production pottery and clay sculpture has culminated in my current work. Spirit and clay, inspiration and method have led to a discovery through process—images and textures on gridlike sections of vitrified clay that I call Murals.

In this book I have tried to answer the many questions people have asked me over the years about my work and my process. I offer this book as a kind of map of the territory I have traveled following the spirit of Living Clay.

So many good people have come into my life at just the right time. Many of the gifts they gave I am still receiving. To acknowledge them all would be a daunting task. I hope I gave as good as I got—and am forever grateful for the experience.

Special thanks to the following for help with this book: my family for gently jogging my memory and providing unfailing encouragement; Jack Kotz, the talented photographer who shot glyphs and studio, kiln and work, always insisting on the very best light, no matter what the weather conditions; David Padilla, my studio assistant for his good humor and great skill; to Sheila Cowing for her expertise and honesty in editing; Robert Levin for magically keeping my temperamental computer working; Nancy Fay for her persistence; and Judith Asher, my publisher, for her vision and commitment to detail.

Please note: In Galisteo the glyphs and clay deposits are all located on private property, sacred and protected. Being on this land has been a great personal privilege, but as these are private places, well marked with No Trespassing signs, I can only share the story with you.

# 1

# ORIGINS

had the good fortune to grow up in Santa Fe. I have early memories of an old adobe house on East Garcia Street. The walls were softly curved and the tall narrow window panes were painted with animal designs in lieu of curtains. The doors were colored Taos blue to keep evil spirits away, and the hand-forged hinges squeaked loudly when opened. Wooden furniture, handmade in Mexico, was padded with colorful weavings and soft curly sheepskins. It was a simple environment, crafted with skill, shaped by necessity. When we lived in this house in 1940, rent was twelve dollars a month.

The Santa Fe of my childhood was quite different from today. World War II was ending; artists, soldiers, ladies, and ladies of the evening, expatriates, politicians—rounders of all kinds—were moving here. Santa Fe truly was the end of the trail, a land of opportunity for those wanting to forget the past and start a new life.

Local people were mostly Spanish or Indian. There were not many Anglos, and Anglo children were a real minority. There were very few tourists and we called them visitors. Los Alamos, buzzing with PhD's, was an open secret in town and, as we were to learn, home to a spy or two. Wounded soldiers recovering at the Veterans' Hospital (now the College of Santa Fe) were a common sight. I remember going with my father to visit our neighbor, Kurt Schram, the German watchmaker, while he was imprisoned in the German-Japanese internment camp located near Alameda Street. He repaired pocket watches and grandfather clocks, and my father delivered the money he earned to his wife and children.

*Age 6*
*Santa Fe Plaza*

My family grew a victory garden, received ration stamps for sugar and gasoline, and saved tin cans to recycle for the war effort. As a child I felt our greatest sacrifice was sending the family dog, an Airedale named Bishop, to serve in the K9 corps. When the war ended Bishop came home, but he always attacked the postman and any one else who wore a uniform. We were unable to retrain him and we reluctantly sent him away again, this time permanently.

In 1944 my parents divorced. My mother, Rosalea Murphy, is herself an artist and most of her friends were painters and

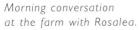

*Morning conversation at the farm with Rosalea.*

sculptors. She moved here from New Orleans seeking a creative life. Faced with the necessity of earning a living, she combined her love of entertaining with a talent for cooking and opened a small restaurant, The Pink Adobe. The first menu was modest—onion soup and apple pie. The walls were hung with her latest paintings; candles stuck in wine bottles burned late into the night while ideas and liquor flowed freely. Her innovative restaurant grew to become one of the creative energies that has shaped Santa Fe for fifty-five years, too large a legend to relate here.

My father, Bob Stephens, was a local politician and lobbyist for the liquor dealers' association, which had become very active now that Prohibition had ended. His office was downtown in Sena Plaza, but he lived five miles from town in Tesuque. He and his new wife had two horses, and I spent summers in the Sangre de Cristo Mountains, riding bareback on a pinto horse. My new step-sister Cathy and I knew all the gates, streams, and Forest Service trails that led to the Ski Basin. They became as familiar as downtown streets and plaza shops in quickly growing Santa Fe.

I grew up shuttled between my father's and my mother's two very different worlds; their eclectic friends were painters, politicians, cowboys, and intellectuals. I learned to love animals, art, good conversations, and nature, but my passion for clay was a little unexpected—although there were a few early clues.

I remember a potter named Bud Gilbertson who was Rosalea's friend. He had traveled the world extensively and studied pottery in Japan. He lived in a sort of Third World way—very close to his animals and work.

He had very little money and his studio was an open shed outside in the back yard where he made pottery with clay dug from the clay pit on Cerro Gordo Road. He glazed his work with a traditional Japanese Chun blue glaze made with fireplace ashes and plasterer's lime. It amazed me that he could make something so beautiful from ordinary dirt and ashes.

He served hot wine in handmade cups and showed us his new work, wind bells, that he thumped with his fingers to let us hear the sound of a good ringing clay.

*Backyard with my dog, Cerro Gordo, and geese*

He loved ducks, and a flock of them lived freely in the kiln yard. Their quacking and the bells' chiming fascinated me. I never worked with him; I was from another generation, and he died years before I became involved with clay. But now there are many questions I wish I could ask him. I think we would have a good conversation.

Looking back, I know he gave me a first glimpse of the alchemy that I would come to value.

The first time I saw a potter making a large bowl on a potter's wheel, I had a strange feeling of familiarity, a sense of recognition so strong it was almost a physical reaction. This was something I thought I could do—would do. And it was, but it took some time.

By 1964 Canyon Road was a haven for young painters and craftsmen, but very few were interested in pottery or knew much about clay and firing. I was fortunate to have a neighbor who was a potter. Pat Patterson and I became friends, and he would let me try working some clay on his wheel. He ate his lunch in peace and quiet while I kept his shop open, sold an occasional coffee mug or weed pot, and struggled to center those first lumps of clay.

Learning to throw on Pat's wheel, I would work the clay until it became nothing but goo. Long before my hour of practice was over, the wheel, the floor, my clothes, and who knows what else were splattered and drenched with clay. I would mop up and then put the wet clay on a plaster bat. Overnight the bat would absorb the excess moisture so I could begin again the next day with that intractable lump.

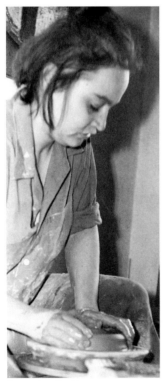

*Learning to throw*

Slowly, over that summer, my fingers learned, and the clay became easier to handle. My feeling began to extend deep into the ball of spinning clay. I learned to center the clay; it began to follow my hands. Lumpy forms began to take on recognizable shapes.

I practiced making the same form again and again, a cylinder, of course—it is the basic form to learn. With every try came a new opportunity to make something that had balance and life. I made rows and rows of cylinders and cut most of them in half to examine wall thickness and evenness. I kept the best ones to track my progress and to have something to show for my efforts. I practiced this one shape and size until I was sure I could produce it every time.

My vocabulary of forms grew. As I gained the skill to handle clay I discovered my voice with every shape I made my own. I favored bowl forms, trying many variations of generous round shapes. Then I went on to pitchers with handles and fitted lids. Finally I mastered plates and platters.

*I discovered my voice with every shape I made my own.*

I had fallen in love with clay. There was no other road for me now.

By this time I was a single mother with two children, Joseph and Denise Louise. The children attended Acequia Madre School, just four blocks from our house, and I worked at my mother's restaurant, The Pink Adobe. I made pots in my spare time, and to my delight these pots sold quickly and brought in extra money.

Encouraged by friends and small successes, I quit my waitress job, installed a small electric kiln and a potter's wheel in one corner of our kitchen, and set to work. First I made sugar bowls, cream pitchers, and coffee mugs. Soon I was selling pottery designed especially for the regional food I loved. Locals and tourists were discovering New Mexican cuisine served on custom-designed enchilada plates, fresh salsa and chip platters, and green chile ramekins. They drank margaritas served up in a special pitcher designed with a lid that held half a fresh lime and a little loose salt.

Folk pottery influenced my work and I frequented antique shops and museums looking for new ideas and old methods I could make my own.

I tried my hand at salt-glazed beer mugs, fluted pie pans, and plates decorated with a traditional cobalt blue slip. Mustache mugs and snuff bottles were a little out of fashion, but I made a few.

In a private collection in Santa Fe, I saw some wonderful jars that had been made in a remote

*Kim Chee Jar,
1975, by Hoback*

mountain village in South Korea. These large storage jars were made to hold pickled and preserved food. Over the summer they would be buried up to their necks in the ground to keep the pickling process cool. They were filled with vegetables, mostly cabbage, then covered with a strong brine and spices and secured by a snug clay lid. These vegetables were eaten with every meal as a relish.

*These big jars
got to me.*

I learned the name of this dish was Kim Chee.
These foreign jars were made to hold a food I had never
tasted. They were dark, rough, and smelled funny. Some of
the rims were chipped and lids were missing. They had been
dug up and traveled a great distance. Korea was an ancient
culture half the world away, a distant continent where we
were fighting a war I did not understand.

But these big jars got to me.

Eastern ideas and aesthetics flowed from those jars into
my Western world. I became a willing pupil. These old pots
were examples of honest beauty that contained natural
imperfections. This was a new idea to me—unadorned
material in skillful hands revealing inner beauty—an exciting
and complex idea.

I investigated Zen, marriage to an airplane pilot, and many
new friends. My work began to change, as did the way I
looked at the world.

And yes, I drank and served hot sake wine from little round
cups I made.

# 2

# HAND

n 1966 I expanded the pottery business to include a retail sales shop. A hand-painted sign beside the front door read "The Pot Shop—942 Canyon Road—Visitors Welcome." The living room was transformed into a pottery store with an antique brass cash register that sat by the front door. A homemade kiln named Pluto filled most of the back yard.

I became a production potter, sales person, and shipping clerk and learned to run a small business, taxes and all. Dinner services, outdoor fountains, bathroom sinks, and wall lamps were designed as customers watched pots being thrown and kilns unloaded. This was what you could call an "earn as you learn" situation.

The ecology movement of the late Sixties created a new consciousness and my friends were turning away from the rush to modernize. Many were dropping out and looking for a simpler way to make a living. Some tried pottery, and my Pot Shop family grew to include other potters, an assistant, several apprentices, and many students.

Here are some ideas, methods, and formulas that worked well over the years.

*Ideas,
methods,
and formulas*

The first lesson always began the same way, with a handful of clay and simple tools. "All you need to start with," I would tell beginners, "is a knife and fork and maybe an apron. Then dig in." Potter's clay changes shape quickly when you begin to form it.

A dialogue begins.

*Hands ask,
clay responds.*

Hands ask, clay responds. This is the language of touch. The thumb pushes a shallow depression in the center of a clay ball, then fingers make gentle pinch, then a small rotation, pinch again; the shape changes. All the way around the pot once, and now again, another round of pinches. A dance begins. Brain to fingers, touch to clay, clay's response to fingers, back to brain. Feedback.

Use the best clay possible. Every clay is improved by aging for ninety days or more. Be patient. Famous potters of the Sung Dynasty prepared clay for future generations.

Clay is processed through a pug mill—a large augur or screw that thoroughly mixes and extrudes the clay. Lumps, air bubbles, inconsistent textures, and whatever other goblins may be lurking there are all smoothed out in this process.

*Clay Mixer*

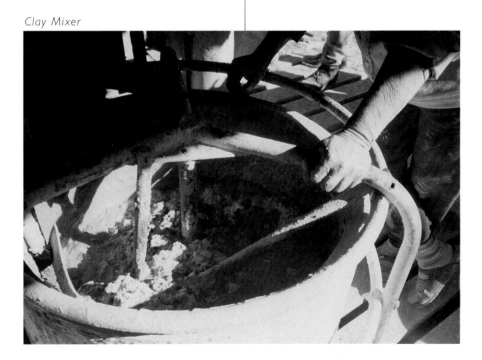

Wheel throwing clay is superior if wedged by hand. Wedging (kneading) literally turns the clay inside out as it stretches and makes clay molecules elastic. Learning to wedge clay is a wonderful moving meditation, a warm up, and allows time to center one's thoughts.

When throwing pots I use an old Randall kick wheel with a 95-pound fly wheel, allowing me a choice between foot and motor power as well as the ability to reverse the turning direction when decorating or trimming.

*Learning to wedge clay is a wonderful moving meditation, a warm up, and allows time to center one's thoughts.*

*Throwing*

*Search for the*
*perfect clay*

My search for the perfect clay started when I bought the first five-pound bag of clay from the local craft store. Soon I was creating my own blend, using hundred-pound bags of fire clays. One day, I mixed in a little dirt from my driveway with a commercially prepared clay that felt like bubble gum. At the time this idea seemed drastic, but it did improve the clay body and start me down the road to using native clays.

I first explored local clay by digging in the abandoned clay pits on Cerro Gordo Road in Santa Fe. This old mine had been worked by penitentiary inmates who made the common red bricks and paving tiles that still cover many of Santa Fe's older sidewalks, as on East De Vargas Street, for example. I never met anyone who had worked there or knew the kilns, but the old pits and salt-fired bricks revealed secrets when studied carefully. This was my source of clay for many years until the property was sold to developers. Now the hillside is built up with fashionable east side homes.

To process the local materials I invested in some small-scale mining equipment. I bought a commercial clay mixer, a hammer mill for grinding native clays, and a shaking screen and ball mill to refine glaze materials. Thirty years later I am still using this equipment.

A little bit about glazes…

Glazes are a thin skin of melted glass covering the clay. They are made by combining minerals into a formula that will melt at a predetermined temperature. Molecular glaze chemistry is an exact science and making good glazes that fit the clay body can be tricky. Formulas must be correctly balanced. If the mix is too refractory, for example, the glaze remains dry and unmelted; too much flux and it runs off into a puddle. Hundreds of glaze formulas are available that will produce almost any color and texture desired.

I chose to work with one basic glaze, experimenting with all the variations that one glaze can yield. I believe this is an elegant solution to developing an individual style.

I loved this glaze on dinnerware and serving dishes—shades and tones harmonize, mix and match, blend and weave from one pot to another, one kiln load to the next. This dinnerware was equally beautiful when empty or generously filled with food.

*Using all the varieties one glaze is capable of producing is an elegant solution toward a individual style.*

Contrasting color for brush work decoration:

Mix 1 tsp mineral oxide into one cup clay slip. Use iron oxide for brownish red or cobalt carbonate for blue.

Over the years I have used three basic glazes—Eggshell (a basic off-white), Piñon Ash (transparent sky blue), and Irresponsible Blue (alligator skin green/black). When mixed with water to the consistency of cream, these glazes are quite opaque. When thinned to pour like milk, they are transparent and showcase the contrasting colors of brush-work designs.

*Ash and iron glaze*

I was determined to make a beautiful ash glaze like Bud Gilbertson's, but ash from my living room fireplace proved a bit unpredictable. One Christmas the burned wrapping papers created most unusual colors.

Piñon Ash Glaze:

| | |
|---|---|
| potash feldspar | 40% |
| washed ash | 40% |
| ball clay | 20% |
| rutile 4% (optional) | |

*Cerro Gordo clay*
*and Piñon Ash glaze*

When I had made enough pots and wanted a change of pace, I would pack up my family and dogs and go to a nearby craft fair. This was a combination working vacation and camping trip. We were like a tribe of gypsies, wheeling and dealing, selling and trading all the pots before we came home with money and new treasures.

*1972 Craft Fair*

At the tender age of six, my daughter Denise was quite articulate and friendly and told stories and answered questions about each and every pot I had made. She was a terrific salesman, and her favorites were little Raku fired pots sculpted into the forms of tropical fish. Gleaming with iridescent colors, they swam through the tree branches behind my display table.

We sold mugs filled with red wine and gave away homemade bread nestled in the large bowls. We awarded prizes to the man with the longest mustache, the blondest girl, and the prettiest baby. The extended family band of banjo and fiddle players entertained with folk songs, and the pots sold quickly. The day I traded my largest bread bowl to a Taos Indian for the drum he had made, I knew I was succeeding artistically.

*The morning air smelled of fresh coffee and sunlight…*

Many kinds of trading went on at these weekend fairs. We shared information, ideas, and customers. There was a certain handcrafted style and Southwestern look beginning to find its way into the mainstream market of decorators and galleries. We had not quite made it yet, but there was great freedom in this lifestyle, and rewards beyond money.

At home I would start early in the morning, making pots for the shop and filling custom orders. Throwing began while it was still quiet. Soon a few visitors would arrive with conversation and gossip. The morning air smelled of fresh coffee and sunlight and I felt somewhat like a village baker from another dimension. Pottery sold while still hot from the kiln, gobbled up like pastries, leaving shelves empty, only to fill again early the next morning with a new batch.

*Production bowls—
one day's work.*

The house was crowded with people and busy with customers, the pottery all-consuming, my children growing into teenagers. Money was always a little tight, but our lives were filled with exciting ideas, good friends, home cooked dinners, and terrific musicians. These were good times for me, times of great adventure and discovery. Seemingly endless kiln loads of pots were made and fired. Once sold, these pots went far and wide, emissaries creating connections that let the unfolding world come in.

I learned that handmade pots go far beyond function in our consciousness and lives; with use they expose deep feelings. Clay is a most intimate material and its familiarity meets quiet needs. People respond to the small chosen artifacts that they use in daily life. Among a set of mugs, one will become a favorite even if we do not fully understand why. Clay pots are personal both to the maker and the user. I think this is why they are treasured far beyond their common clay and domestic function. They become like old friends, familiar and reliable, but difficult to replace if broken.

*Clay is a most intimate material and its familiarity meets quiet needs.*

Twenty years of making production pottery on Canyon Road flew by. So many wonderful friends, students, apprentices, and customers shared those wild years with my family. They watched and asked questions and helped with the work. They sustained and encouraged me as I learned about form following function and change creating new forms.

By 1977, my marriage had ended, Joseph and Denise were away in school, and I had made enough functional pottery—made what felt like millions of pots. I was ready to explore something new, other aspects of work and life. I fell in love again and began a new relationship.

I wanted to move to the country and do country things—have some horses and grow a big garden. The little voice in my head kept saying, "if not now, when?"

# 3

# SPIRIT

n the village of Galisteo I bought a beautiful property
that was originally a sheep ranch headquarters. It had
old rock walls, big cottonwood trees by a creek
and an adobe hacienda. Here, close to the clay I knew,
was the farm and magic I needed. This was the place for me.
I christened it Quartermill Farm. The oldest buildings date
from the Civil War, but most were built in the late 1800s
and were in various degrees of disrepair. The largest empty
building had served as the community wool warehouse, then
later as a dance hall. We supplied the vital juices of electricity,
heat, and plumbing, and repaired the roof. This became my
new studio.

We transformed one of
the stone outbuildings
for the three new mares
and their expected foals.
Joseph came home to
help us raise the big
beams of the horse barn
and lay bricks for the
new kilns. I planted an
asparagus bed, some
herbs, and a small
orchard. Dogs, ducks,
and chickens completed the picture.

*Barn and garden*

Now my time was a mixture of home, studio, gallery, garden,
and farm—one long intertwined process.

*Studio gallery*

The Galisteo farm turned out to be a larger move
than I could have anticipated. I had come here from
busy Canyon Road with the street full of people to
a seemingly empty desert valley. I was eager to live
in the old rambling house with my new love and my
new plans for a country life.

*Much of what
I know of spirit
I have learned here
in the Galisteo Basin.*

I had never thought much about this place—it was so familiar, taken for granted. Like the Zen koan "Who do you ask about the water?" and the answer, "not the fish," I could only see with accustomed eyes. New Mexico is known as the land of enchantment, and I had grown up under her spell. Now I began to discover what was really here. I began to see another point of view, one with new possibilities, perhaps deeper ways of work and connection.

The scope of the land and sky and the cavernous size of my studio changed the scale of my work. I sold large pots—I called them "tribal sized"—at Fenn Gallery in Santa Fe.

*Priscilla looking at glyphs*

Customers or visitors were no longer a constant interruption. My mind moved further from the convenience of town, and my heart moved toward the beauty of the natural world. I was free to think long thoughts as I worked through the day.

Much of what I know of spirit I have learned here in the Galisteo Basin.

I first came here because of the geology. The surrounding mountains are honeycombed with historic mines: gold, silver, turquoise, tin, lead, coal, and, most important to me, clay mines.

Long hikes and picnics to explore the area were the beginning of seeing this place with new eyes.

The valley basin is rimmed by mountains capped with jagged rocks. This rock formation, called a hogback, meanders and curves like the spine of a prehistoric dragon that encircles, defines, and guards. Only a few rough trails lead over and around the rocks to the ridge top. Up here are ancient lookout spots that provide soaring views, horizon to horizon.

*The light is intense and fluid. Strong winds are forever blowing changes and the night sky is very close.*

*Plumed serpent and warrior shield*

As far as the eye can see the land stretches out, undulating with memories of the ancient inland sea that shaped this place.

The south-facing sides of many large rocks are covered with works of ancient artists. Stars, moons, and fierce warrior faces speak a visual language that has never been fully translated. Some think these give directions to a new land and mark its territory, others say these were warnings of dangers to come. Curious images depicting celestial influences have been interpreted many ways, as space travelers, visitations from angels, or forgotten prophesies.

*Galisteo basin looking east*

I have to remember to soften my eyes—it takes a certain kind of peripheral focus before I can see into the little intimate places deep between rock crevices. Patterns of color and eroded shale join together as sunlight plays on images that move in and out of shadow. Stories are recorded, changed, and then erased by time and the forces of wind and rain.

Pecked into the stone's surface
is a virile image of Kokopelli, the
humpbacked flute player. I hear
his song in this windy place as he
plays to the many glyphs representing females and fertility.

Farther to the west, chipped into
the natural rock walls, are three
amazing petroglyphs of Quetzalcoatl, the Plumed Serpent.
This powerful Toltec/Mayan god originated in the jungles
of the Yucatan, and these northernmost images show that
his territory extended north all the way to the Galisteo
Basin. The large snake glyphs stretch a full thirty feet, his
body zig-zagging over many rocks, some now fallen. All three
snakes have large plumes on their heads and warning rattles
on their tails. I walk by lightly and with awe.

Approaching bear glyphs I can almost feel the presence of
some ancient Bear Clan elders. They carved these powerful
images and used them in their healing ceremonies. I feel
at home here, for bears are a recurring theme in my dreams
and in my work.

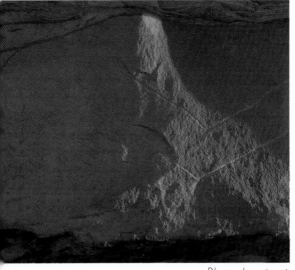

*Plumed serpent*

Nearby spiral glyphs that look like pinwheels have been translated as representing "the journey to the center." This phrase became my personal mantra—this place a metaphorical guide that moves me inward on a journey of self discovery with the awareness that I am the one being mined and shaped and dreamed.

To create works equal in power and spirit to the treasures that others before me left here in the eroding desert is a humbling job. Time and the elements add character and truth to human works that are difficult to find in something newly made. But the urge to make a life in this timeless place is as compelling as ever, and I feel inspired to bring forth images and manifest ideas that are here now.

*Mama bear glyph*

# 4

# HEART

During the first summers in Galisteo, I hosted an annual workshop for potters. For me these seminars were almost family reunions. I had moved off the beaten path—away from Santa Fe's bustling art center—and this was an opportunity to be with old friends, meet new students, and share ideas about the ways of clay and life. The studio was large enough for conversations and demonstrations, and there was a camping place by the Galisteo Creek for the more adventurous participants.

Some of the teachers—Michael Cardew, Peter Volkus, Karen Karnes, and Paul Soldner—had led workshops at the Pot Shop and were my mentors. There were not many "do it yourself" books on ceramics then—these were the teachers who would write them. My favorite was Michael Cardew's new book *Pioneer Pottery,* and I was following it like a bible. He was a strong advocate and authority for using local materials.

Having these expert teachers and fellow clay workers here in my new studio was the timely encouragement I needed. They generously shared their experiences and technical information and gave me courage. Building this new world challenged my resources and energies.

*Maria Martinez, Adam Martinez, and Michael Cardew*

*Cardew teaching*

There are always demonstrations at workshops, and watching one of these masters throw a pot on a wheel is inspiring. A shape appears to just grow. A hollow three-dimensional form rises as trained hands support the soft walls and press upward, carefully guiding the vortexing shape. The elastic clay is stretched and raised until the final form is achieved through an intricate dance of mind and motion.

*Clay wall*

Technically, skill is skill—but this process might be compared to cooking, making hollandaise sauce for instance. The recipe is simple—egg yolk, butter, and lemon juice—but it's a light hand, flawless timing, and talent that creates the memorable sauce.

As part of the workshops we hiked to the clay deposits. Using raw materials instead of the commercially available clays was an appealing idea to many potters. Even those who were not fond of my methods of extensive testing and record keeping were fascinated by the idea of returning to the source.

Later, around the campfire, we offered our opinions and experience with clay and exchanged advice. There are many varieties of clay on the market. Commercial clay has been ground, sifted, and washed but is not sold with working instructions printed on the bag. It can even be difficult to get the chemical formula from the manufacturer. Information about firing or vitrifying temperatures, shrink rates, and dry strengths can be measured, but the quality of forming in the hand is subjective.

Availability of materials is forever changing. There was a time, for instance, when the only use for uranium was as a glaze colorant that produced a beautiful yellow.

*Galisteo Creek*

In these workshops, craftsmanship and inspiration are passed on, one to one, and hand to hand. This is the alchemical process of turning clay to gold—all the many kinds of gold.

*Testing the clay:
the unusual beauty and
energy of accidents*

I settled in to the new studio and began serious clay testing. Ideas developed—and the work changed. In the kiln melting minerals flashed into brilliant colors that flowed and formed bubbles and rough craters. Sometimes the clay warped and bloated, overheated into strange shapes. But the unusual beauty and energy of these accidents cried out to find a format that would showcase these seemingly destructive accidents. Unloading the kiln was an adventure, turning still warm pots carefully, looking for the effects new clays might cause. I always wanted to enlarge and feature these effects.

I experimented with combinations of clays and arroyo sand for texture that were rolled into thin slabs. These pieces were carefully marked with identifying numbers. Increasing the size of these slabs in two inch increments revealed the material's limits. I was thrilled with the maximum fired size, 25 x 12 inches more or less.

I sculpted the slab's underside with my fingers raising furrows or making small stretch marks and surface tears. Wanting more dimension still, I curled and overlapped edges. Surface cracks or imperfections echoed natural forces; these fired slabs looked much like the wall of an arroyo.

I began to see color in a new way—and stopped glazing in the traditional manner. Wanting a dryer, more natural look, I brushed undiluted minerals directly onto and into clay. Instead of sealing the surface, color became a mottled layer like the oxidized face of rocks. Saturated colors are made by concentrating the pure minerals—the more used, the brighter the color. This is somewhat like working with watercolors, which are also pure pigment.

I did not know if oxides would fuse into the clay without the addition of glaze flux. They did.

Test pieces accumulated in the studio: slabs of clay painted with formulas and dates, maps and directions, and sketches of a few memorable incidents. They became a clay-to-stone record of how the work was progressing. Several are still hanging here, including one favorite plaque of a mother pea hen and her five baby chicks. Picking just the texture and color I wanted, some dark and sandy, some as spotted as bobcats, I would draw and color on the clay's surface. These drawings expanded to include dreams, stories, and Chinese zodiac animals.

*I began
to see color
in a new way.*

Now I had a color palette:

copper and cobalt
made blue

vanadium and rutile
made yellow

cadmium made red
and orange

iron made black and brown

Suddenly ideas began to jell and I knew I was on to something.

I am self taught, have not studied formally, and perhaps

this freedom allowed me to trust my own way of working.

Perhaps this process was the end result of a move away

from a busy community into the open space of the desert

where ideas were internalized and grew quickly when

connected with heart feelings.

*San Isidro plaque*

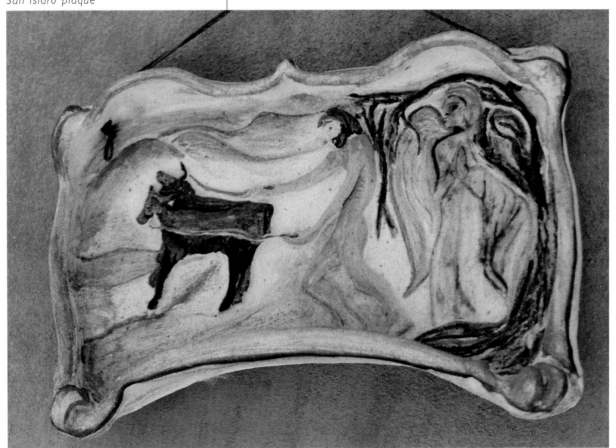

# 5

# VOICE

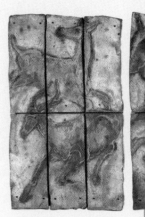
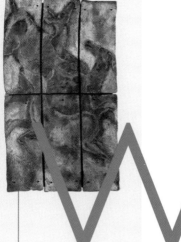

While showing these new works to friends, we searched for a word to call them, one name that described this combination of images, indigenous clays, and the effects of fire.

The search continues, as they are not really paintings or drawings, and calling them clay paintings leaves out the catalyst of firing. I know technically they are not murals, clay reliefs, or sculpture, but, lacking a better idea, I continue to call them Murals.

The murals are visual stories telling of familiar animals and unusual experiences that have quickened my heartbeat with fear or love. Some are from dream time and half-remembered images when humans, animals, gods, and the elements lived without hierarchy. Others are personal myths from kingdoms of alchemical minerals and symbolic animals, fused together into one totality.

*Bear glyph with graffiti*

Imagined ceremonies, blessings, and teachings are intriguing subjects, as is living here on the farm with eight horses, three dogs, a pet raven, a parrot, and a flock of chickens, endless opportunities to observe mischief and become inspired.

Ideas begin like smoke, leave a faint scent and a few tracks—the hunt begins.

*The hunt begins.*

Whenever I climb the hogback, I visit the bear glyphs. Over the years one has been badly disfigured as travelers marked their arrival with Spanish crosses, cattle brands, and their initials—adding another layer of history to the rock face, another sign of changing territory.

One night a few years ago I dreamed that a starry bear stepped down from the sky onto Cerro Pelon Mountain. This huge old bear's back and rump curved just the way the mountain does. I watched closely, but all I could see was the mountain's familiar shape against the Milky Way; mountain and bear had silently merged. Later I watched the Big Dipper's rotation across the night sky and remembered the name Ursa Major, Big Bear. I use the color turquoise to symbolize the sky bear's descent, the heaven's connection to the earth, sacredness and healing. The word *bear* has a number of meanings—to expose, endure or create—adding to the dimension and mood I use in this series.

*Ursa Major and Ursa Minor*

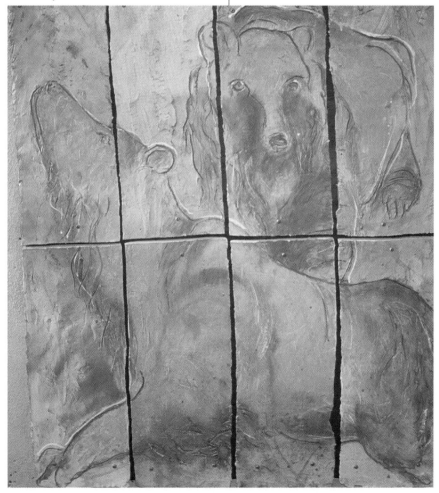

Petroglyphs, oral stories, and local legends tell of a connection and affection between the land and the animals.

One such story is from Old Bird Woman of the Kiowas. When the buffalo herds were slaughtered, a way of life ended. The Chief Buffalo went to the Great Spirits for help. These spirits caused the mountain to break open; all the buffalo vanished safely inside, then the mountain closed, leaving a vast emptiness. The mountain Bird Woman tells of is Mount Scott in Oklahoma.

To my way of thinking, this mountain is the human heart. With a remembered vision of this land containing the abundance of wilderness, I think that mountain opens. I feel that abundance in my heart while horseback riding

*Affection between*
*the land and*
*the animals*

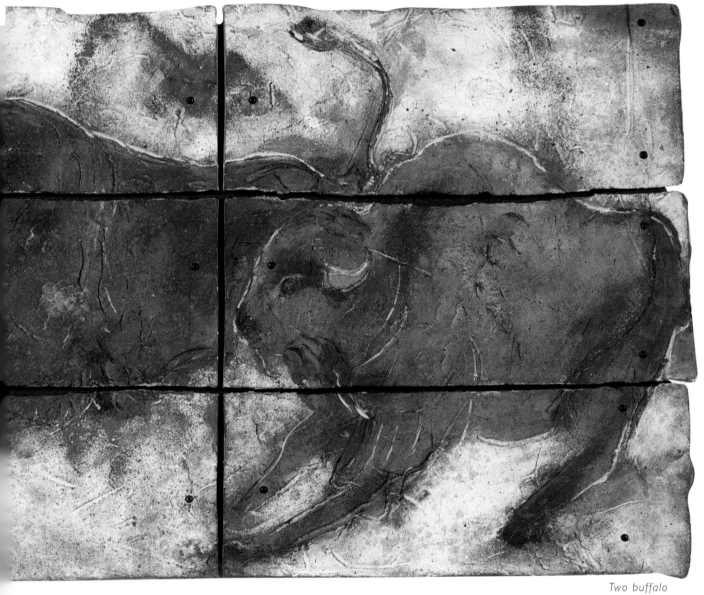

*Two buffalo*

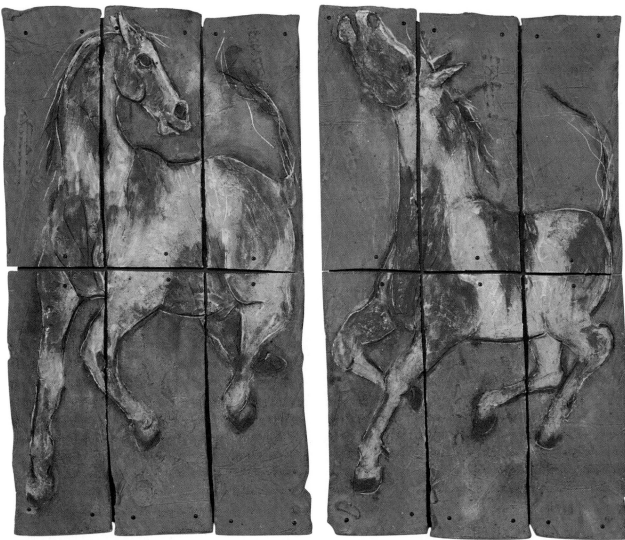

*My Father's Horse*

through open land with blowing rustling grasses. The undulations of the land echo the ancient inland sea and the great herds. The sea and the buffalo are gone, and their absence here leaves a vacuum that fills with humpbacked ghost shadows and lowing calls on the wind.

I find horses visually exciting, the image of a horse running, silhouetted against the sky, deeply moving. This agility of motion and elegance of form embodies pure spirit.

When I ride, I feel the changing balance of four feet beneath me and know the way bones and muscles work together. I feel energy and rhythm, and this kinesthetic knowledge influences my drawing. I do not portray my individual animals, but rather impressions of motion and the emotion they create.

One series of murals, *My Father's Horse*, was inspired by accounts of early Spaniards trekking north and Comanche Indians stealing their ponies blended with memories of the black and white pinto pony I first rode.

*Priscilla on Navajo*

*For a time the studio may
be full of white deer,
and then those fade out.
As work on another idea begins,
I am in a land of herons
or antelope,
thinking their thoughts.*

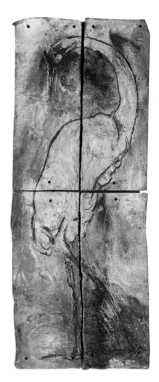

Whooping Cranes

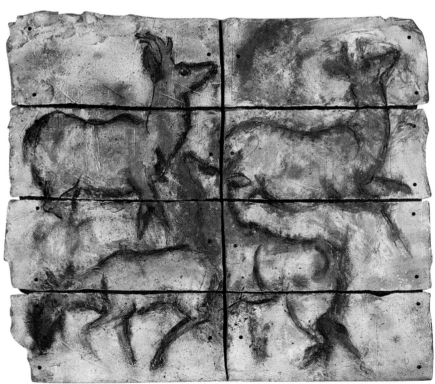

Antelope

*The murals are
visual stories,
telling of familiar
animals and unusual
experiences that
have quickened
my heartbeat with
fear or love.*

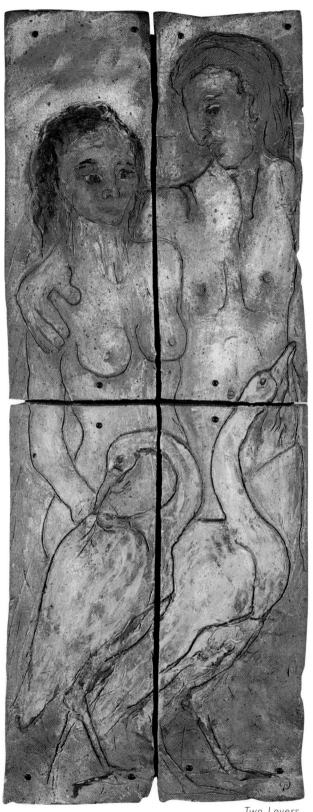

*Two Lovers*

With loose ideas of image, texture, color, shape, and size, I begin the composition. The clay is my canvas and I draw directly on it with my fingers, a bamboo pen, or a plasterer's trowel. The wet clay surface is responsive to every impression. I must draw quickly because uncovered clay begins to dry rapidly. Surfaces cannot be overworked lest they become muddy and lose vitality.

*Pulling*

Color is brushed on large areas, new lines and other colors added, places scraped away, layers built up and broken down, revealing a cycle—create and destroy—as the surface changes. Each new layer registers impressions like a window to a single geological time.

Before the clay dries completely, I cut the modular units to size and punch the screw holes that will secure the mounted sections.

*Painting*

Marketing new work is always challenging, presenting many questions, some aesthetic, some technical, and some architectural. It required several years of experimentation before finding how best to display, transport, and install these murals.

*Painting*

Mounting:

Plywood is cut, shaped, sealed, and painted. Heavy-duty picture hanger wire is countersunk into the back side of the plywood.

Foam cushions are placed between clay and plywood. Screws secure the clay slabs to the plywood backing. The mural's weight is about the same as that of a mirror of equal size.

*Installation of White Deer by David Padilla*

# 6

# FIRE

Firing the kiln begins the next phase of the creation process. If I had to choose just one job in the cycle of making pottery that best fits my nature, I would choose to fire the kiln.

I have deep love and respect for kilns, finding them combinations of dragon, slave, and ancient god—mysterious and temperamental.

Each firing varies a little, sensitive to the way the kiln is
stacked, the types of glazes used, and sometimes the weather.
But all of the pots in one kiln load are like siblings and have
the same molecular structure, resembling each other no
matter whose hand formed the clay. The next firing will be
slightly different, so the next
batch of pots will be a little
different, somewhat like
conditions in the garden—
season after season.

*Shelves, plates, Volkos pot*

I made the first kiln for the
shop on Canyon Road from a
mixture of fire clay, vermiculite,
and ground-up apricot pits.
This thick mud was slump molded over a plywood form. It
looked sort of like a dog house with bricks stacked at the
open ends to form the back wall and front door. The burner
consisted of two tubes welded together at right angles. The
top tube dripped kerosene into the bottom tube that was
attached to a blower, my vacuum cleaner. It sounded like a
jet engine, and it would fire up to cone 10 in three hours if
encouraged by opening the fuel valve wide.

*Building the new kiln*

*Fired cones*

The kiln I am using now is the product of a more modern technology. It is made of insulating bricks and fired with venturi burners, but it too was homemade, with the kind help of a potter friend, Dick Masterson. The walls are a double layer of brick encased in a steel frame. The roof is flat and spanned with bricks strung on stainless steel rods, shiskabob style. The freestanding chimney is made of fire bricks stacked twenty feet tall and secured with guy wires. This high tech dragon is fueled with propane gas, stored in two 500 gallon tanks. When asked what fuel I use, I answer, dollar bills. Alas, it is almost true.

I fire the kiln about twice a month and each firing takes several days. Loading a kiln has a geometry all its own; it's a three dimensional jigsaw puzzle of clay pieces, silicon carbide shelves, and brick stilts. Pots are stacked to the top of the kiln; every possible space is filled. A wall of bricks closes the door and large cracks are sealed with soft clay. There are two carefully placed "peep holes" in the top and bottom of the door so I can look inside the kiln during firing to see the cones, the clay thermometers. Burners are carefully lit and turned up gradually so the pots won't crack from heat shock. About eight hours into the firing, all burners are turned on full blast. Now filled with open flames, the kiln makes a sound like a big cat's low growl. I listen carefully because this sound is a guide to what is happening inside. During the firing, flames flow through the kiln like a current of water between stones in a river. The kiln smells of white hot molecules hungry for oxygen, another clue to what is going on inside and when to adjust the air and gas mixture to produce the desired effects.

At full heat, the interior of the kiln is a bright incandescent white. I wear dark glasses as I look through the peep holes to make out the cones. When they "fatigue," or bend over, the maximum heat has been reached. Burners are turned off; there is a sudden silence, but the heat remains, glowing intensely.

*The pottery ripens in the heat.*

*Unloading sequence*

*Mounting murals*

The temperature slowly begins to drop. The interior glow changes from bright white to yellow—down to orange and then dark red. By evening of the second day it is quite dark inside the kiln again, but it takes another twenty-four hours before the kiln is cool enough to unbrick the door.

Over the past forty years I have fired many kilns, spending long nights in my back yard trying to create temperatures and atmospheres more at home on some other planet, perhaps the planet Mercury, the closest to our sun. I often think of mythical Mercury the trickster, changing everything around him while remaining unaffected himself.

Keeping watch, I see the sun set; sometimes I see the moon rise and the starry sky brighten with the Milky Way. The day's light fades at about the same rate as the kiln's interior begins to glow with fire. I watch color change as heat rises degree by degree.

These nights inspire me as much as the pottery that ripens in that heat.

# 7

# SOUL

Change in the high desert is constant and quite visible, sometimes more startling than change in a kiln. With every storm the land erodes and new terrain becomes exposed. Familiar trails wear into gullies that soon deepen and become impassable; flash floods widen the arroyos and change their courses. Time and weather are forever rearranging the familiar and presenting the unknown.

On a long summer day like today, Galisteo village looks timeless, as though under enchantment, but it will not stay contained this way very long. Through the apple trees I can hear traffic speeding down old Highway 41, toward the new supermarket ten miles away. Highway 285 is undergoing major construction, being widened to four lanes that will safely accommodate increasing local traffic as well as the environmentally controversial WIPP trucks (Waste Isolation Pilot Project) transporting radioactive waste from Los Alamos to Carlsbad.

I too am being changed by the forces of time: success, unexpected illness and divorce, meaningful work, two wonderful grandchildren, love of good friends, and what I have come to call the adventures of "village life."

I trust and counsel patience while following that spiral to the center and pursuing clay to a new destination.

These days my destination is a very special clay mine. I leave the highway behind and drive down a deeply rutted dirt road that crosses the southwestern corner of a neighboring ranch. This old road curves close to ancient Pueblo Blanco, continues south past an old coal mine, and ends abruptly at an abandoned homestead.

*I trust and counsel patience while following that spiral to the center and pursuing clay to a new destination.*

For the past twenty years these clay deposits had been mined by an Albuquerque brick company that used this clay to make red bricks for the construction of new homes. When the brick manufacturer retired, another dream came true—I was able to buy the property that contained this mine.

Mine strata

Twenty years of strip mining devoured one side of the mountain, creating a cut that is forty feet tall and an amphitheater the length of a football field. The exposed cliff wall looks like the cross section of a Dagwood sandwich, layer after layer of rock, sandstone, clay, and coal. Here is an eye-to-eye view of one hundred million years of geological time—exposing Paleozoic, Mesozoic, and Cenozoic eras.

When it comes to using the earth's materials, I have always been of two minds. My desire to freely explore and use what the earth provides is often at odds with my strong feelings that much of the natural world is being destroyed, perhaps needlessly. Balancing paradise and progress has been a personal challenge, calling me to increased responsibility and awareness.

I work the Pueblo Blanco mine, claiming and reclaiming this place. Walls of the old clay pits have been sloped and graded to catch the seasonal rain runoff. Now there are two large ponds planted with bog plants and stocked with tadpoles and mosquito-eating fish. Around the ponds young cottonwood

*I gather the clay*
*for my work,*
*one mural at a time.*

*Mine panorama*

and willow trees are pushing roots deep into the damp soil. Someday they will provide shade. I gather the clay for my work, one mural at a time.

Antelope drank here at the new pond just yesterday leaving their tracks deep in the soft clay mud. These sharp shapes and a glimpse of wild red and white bodies will be the next subject I pursue.

*The Galisteo Basin*
*continues to share*
*its treasures.*

*Conversation with Ravenheart*

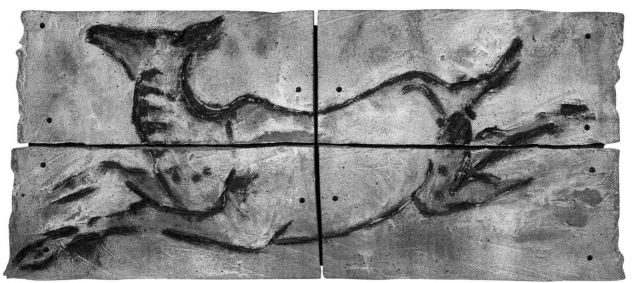

*January Flight*

## ABOUT THE PRESS

Sherman Asher Publishing is an independent literary press publishing fine poetry, memoir, fiction, Judaica, books on writing, and other books we love since 1994. We publish both regional and international voices that engage us and deserve a wider audience. We are dedicated to "Changing the World One Book at a Time."™ Visit our web site at www.shermanasher.com to order our titles.

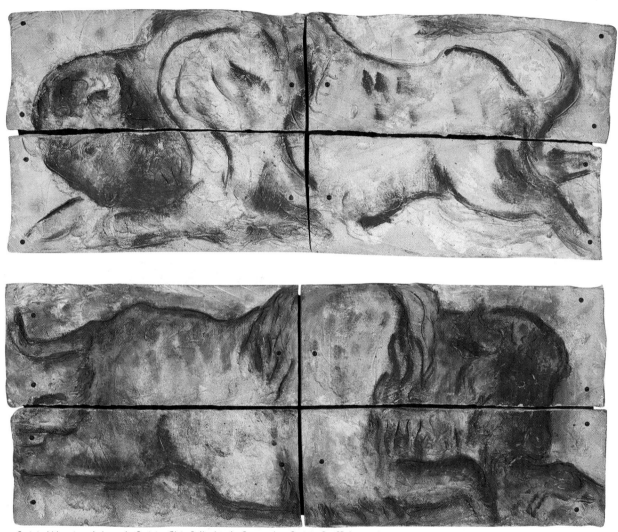

*Spirit Warrior (above), Spirit Chief (below), from the Spirit Buffalo series*